W9-AGJ-863

THE TELEVISION

Richard and Louise Spilsbury

Chicago, Illinois

www.capstonepub.com
Visit our website to find out more information about Heinemann-Raintree books.

To order:
☎ Phone 800-747-4992
▣ Visit www.capstonepub.com
to browse our catalog and order online.

Edited by Louise Galpine and Laura Knowles
Designed by Philippa Jenkins
Illustrations by KJA-artists.com
Original illustrations © Capstone Global Library
    Limited 2012
Illustrated by KJA-artists.com
Picture research by Mica Brancic
Originated by Capstone Global Library Limited
Printed in the United States of America in
Eau Claire, Wisconsin

052518
000562

Library of Congress Cataloging-in-Publication Data
Spilsbury, Richard, 1963-
   The television / Richard and Louise Spilsbury.
      p. cm.—(Tales of invention)
   Includes bibliographical references and index.
   ISBN 978-1-4329-4881-8 (hc)—ISBN 978-1-4329-4890-0 (pb) 1. Television—Juvenile literature. I. Spilsbury, Louise. II. Title.
   TK6640.S65 2012
   621.388—dc22   2010036504

Acknowledgments
We would like to thank the following for permission to reproduce photographs: Alamy pp. **20** (© Interfoto), **27** (© Artur Marciniec); Corbis pp. **4** (Reuters/© Peter Macdiarmid), **10** (© Bettmann), **12** (© Bettmann), **14** (© Bettmann), **15** (© Bettmann), **16** (© Bettmann), **17** (© Bettmann), **18** (© Bettmann), **22** (Reuters/© Hannibal Hanschke), **26** (Blend Images/© Colin Anderson); Getty Images pp. **11** (Hulton Archive/Keystone), **21** (CBS Photo Archive), **24** (Photodisc/Ed Freeman), **25** (Stone/Flying Colors); Library of Congress pp. **8**, **13**; Science Photo Library pp. **5** (Adam Hart-Davis), **9** (RIA Novosti), **7**.

Cover photograph of a woman demonstrating a television set at a radio exhibition in 1938, reproduced with permission of Corbis/© Hulton-Deutsch Collection.

We would like to thank Walter Podrazik for his invaluable help in the preparation of this book.

Every effort has been made to contact copyright holders of material reproduced in this book. Any omissions will be rectified in subsequent printings if notice is given to the publisher.

Disclaimer
All the Internet addresses (URLs) given in this book were valid at the time of going to press. However, due to the dynamic nature of the Internet, some addresses may have changed, or sites may have changed or ceased to exist since publication. While the author and publisher regret any inconvenience this may cause readers, no responsibility for any such changes can be accepted by either the author or the publisher.

CONTENTS

Look for these boxes

Biographies

These boxes tell you about the life of inventors, the dates when they lived, and their important discoveries.

Setbacks

Here we tell you about the experiments that didn't work, the failures, and the accidents.

EUREKA!

These boxes tell you about important events and discoveries, and what inspired them.

Any words appearing in the text in bold, **like this**, are explained in the glossary.

TIMELINE

2011—The timeline shows you when important discoveries and inventions were made.

BEFORE TELEVISION

Most of us take television for granted. We can switch it on at any time to see news, movies, sports, nature programs, and more. But what is television? It is a way of sending and receiving images (pictures) and sounds through wires, air, or space as waves of energy. Television cameras convert action into **signals**, or patterns of **electricity**. The television sets we have in our homes are **receivers**. The receivers convert the electricity back into programs we can see and hear.

Huge, modern TV screens allow large crowds to watch events on television.

1834—William George Horner invents the zoetrope

1837—Samuel Morse demonstrates an electric **telegraph**

Moving pictures at home

Before television was invented, the only moving pictures most people saw were at the movie theater. Only a few people saw moving images at home—for example, using toys such as a zoetrope. The zoetrope is a hollow drum with slits around the edge and a sequence of different images inside. The images look as if they are moving when the viewer spins the drum and looks through the slits from the outside.

In 1997 an estimated 2.5 billion people—nearly half of the world's population—watched the funeral of Diana, Princess of Wales. This was the biggest-ever TV news audience.

What people saw with zoetropes was quite different from what we watch on television today. The development and spread of television took many decades and involved many inventors.

The zoetrope tricks the brain into seeing differences between images as movements of the same image.

In the mid- to late-1800s, people communicated by **telegraph**, which sent words using different **signals** through wires. In 1883 Paul Nipkow invented a way to send images in a similar way, using metal discs with holes in them. Up close, an image, such as a drawing, is made of a pattern of light and dark. **Scanning** converts that pattern, line by line, into a sequence of signals. One **Nipkow disc** scanned an image, while a second disc used the signals to recreate the image.

How a Nipkow disc works

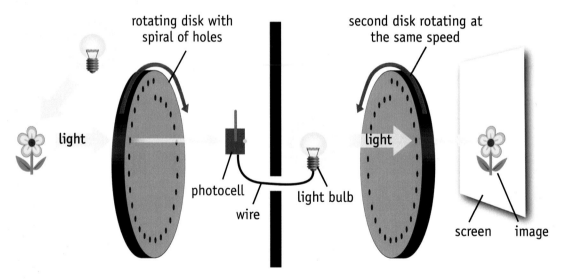

rotating disk with spiral of holes

second disk rotating at the same speed

light

light

photocell

light bulb

wire

screen   image

1. The disc has a spiral pattern of holes. When the disc **rotates**, each hole moves across the image.

2. The amount of light from the image passing through each hole is detected by a **photocell**. This is a special bulb covered with a substance called selenium, which conducts more **electricity** when it is lit up than when dark.

3. The photocell's electrical signal passes through a wire to a bulb, making the bulb glow or remain dark.

4. Light from the bulb shines through a second rotating disc and shows the image on a screen.

Paul Nipkow *(1860–1940)*

German inventor Paul Nipkow was a student when he designed his scanner. The invention sent an image from London, England, to Paris, France. But few people saw a practical use for it. Nipkow spent much of his life as a railroad engineer.

Seeing the invisible

Scientists studying atoms, the tiny building blocks of all matter, realized that they contained **electrons**. But electrons are like moving pieces of electricity that are impossible to see! In 1897 German scientist Ferdinand Braun invented a device called the **cathode ray tube** that could show where electrons were.

The cathode ray tube is a glass tube with no air inside that contains a part called a cathode. When electricity moves through the cathode, it heats up and sends out a beam of electrons through the tube. A spot of light appears at the flat end of the tube. This happens because the glass at that end is painted with a chemical that glows when electrons hit it.

Ferdinand Braun shared the 1909 Nobel Prize for Physics with Guglielmo Marconi, who invented the radio.

Braun used his invention to study electrons, but others realized the cathode ray tube could be used to make televisions.

The next step

Braun then started to experiment with his invention. He discovered that **magnets** could pull or push the electron beam, just as they would an iron bar. Using magnets, he could make the spot of light move to different parts of the screen. Braun also varied the amount of electricity going into the electrode. This changed the size of the electron beam—and therefore the brightness of the light on the screen.

Setbacks

In 1908 British engineer Alan Campbell-Swinton gave a lecture. In it, he said that a cathode ray tube could show complete images made of dots of light sent through wires. However, he never managed to come up with a working model.

9

THE FIRST TELEVISIONS

In 1922 Charles Jenkins invented a way to send images without wires. His system **scanned** images in a similar way to **Nipkow discs**. **Signals** from the scan made **electrons** vibrate in a machine called a **transmitter**.

The electrons produced **radio waves**, which are fast-moving vibrations of energy. Antennae on **receivers** could capture some of the waves. The receiver converted the radio waves back into signals, and then into tiny images on a screen. People viewed these through a built-in magnifying glass. Jenkins famously demonstrated his system in 1923, when he sent an image of President Warren G. Harding 210 kilometers (130 miles) across the United States, from Washington, D.C., to Philadelphia.

Here, Charles Jenkins is showing his equipment, which he claimed could transmit moving images through radio waves.

Baird's breakthrough

On March 25, 1925, Scottish inventor John Logie Baird demonstrated a **mechanical** TV in a large store in London. It showed moving images of drawings scanned with Nipkow discs and transmitted by radio. A few months later, Baird transmitted images of a talking puppet called Stooky Bill from his tiny laboratory. He used a puppet because the lamps used to light up the televised subject (so it could be scanned) were too hot for actors. Even so, Stooky Bill's hair was burned and his lips cracked from the heat!

This is the equipment used to create the tiny, blurred television image of Stooky Bill.

Setbacks

Charles Jenkins claimed to have sent Radio-Movies (moving images as radio waves) in 1923, but there are no reliable records. His first transmission was in June 1925, just three months after Baird!

11

1883—Paul Nipkow invents the Nipkow disc to scan images (see page 6)

1885

1890

John Logie Baird showed how his invention worked by transmitting his own image.

Improvements

After the first television, Baird improved his invention. He used bigger discs with more holes. These scanned images with higher **resolution**, as there were more lines making up the image. The discs **rotated** faster, so images replaced each other more quickly and flickered less on screen. He used **photocells** that needed less light to make a signal, so television could be filmed using weaker, cooler lamps or even daylight. Baird also added a device called an **amplifier**, which made the signal stronger. This meant it could be transmitted farther using radio waves. By 1928 Baird had sent a television signal from London to New York.

1897—J. J. Thomson discovers electrons. Ferdinand Braun invents the **cathode ray tube** (see page 8).

John Logie Baird *(1888–1946)*

In his twenties, John Logie Baird tried to make artificial (fake) diamonds, and he succeeded in inventing socks that helped prevent foot infections. He made his first TV out of materials he found in his laboratory, such as old cookie tins and bike lights!

Electronic television

In 1927 American Philo Farnsworth invented the first completely **electronic** television. Electronic machines work by controlling the flow of electrons, rather than mechanical parts. Farnsworth's TV camera was a **cathode ray tube** with a special screen inside that produced electrons wherever light fell. **Magnets** bent the electrons line by line into a tube that converted them into signals. In the receiver's cathode ray tube, the signals were pieced back into images with 300 lines of resolution. That was 10 times more than Baird's first **broadcasts**.

EUREKA!

Farnsworth was driving a tractor when he invented his TV. He realized that a moving electron beam could scan an image line by line, in a similar way to how he plowed his family's fields.

Philo Farnsworth's electronic television produced a much clearer image than earlier inventions.

Philo Taylor Farnsworth (1906–1971)

Philo Farnsworth decided to invent electrical machines when he was young, living on a farm in Rigby, Idaho. In 1922, at age 14, he decided that Nipkow discs would not move fast enough to scan images, and that moving electrons were the answer. After going to college to learn more, Farnsworth finally built his TV in 1927, with the help of money given by some local businessmen. By then Philo had married his college sweetheart, Pem, who helped him with his invention. She was also the first person ever broadcast on electronic TV!

1920—Charles Jenkins sends still images using radio waves (see page 10)

TELEVISION TAKES OFF

In the late 1920s in the United Kingdom, Baird demonstrated **mechanical** televisions to the public. In the 1930s, the British Broadcasting Corporation (BBC) started **transmitting** television programs using Baird's system. By the early 1930s, thousands of people were watching these programs on television **receivers**.

In the United States, Charles Jenkins helped introduce mechanical televisions. In the late 1920s and early 1930s, members of the public began to buy mechanical televisions. Eventually 42 different television stations were showing programming using Jenkins's system.

Early programs were experiments to see what was possible with the new invention. For example, one of the first stars of U.S. television was a small statue of the cartoon character Felix the Cat **rotating** on a turntable!

Mechanical TV cameras of the 1930s were big, but some could produce very clear images.

1923—Vladimir Zworykin invents the iconoscope

1925—John Logie Baird demonstrates the first working TV to the public. Charles Jenkins transmits his first Radio-Movies (see page 11).

1927—Philo Farnsworth invents the first electronic TV (see page 14)

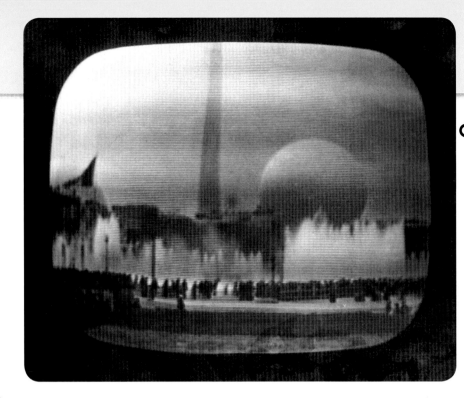

The U.S. public was amazed at the clear images when RCA demonstrated its new electronic TV cameras at the World's Fair in 1939.

Electronic television takes over

During the 1930s, various inventors made **electronic** TV cameras based on Farnsworth's ideas. Isaac Shoenberg created a version that was less bulky and produced better images than Baird's mechanical camera. Vladimir Zworykin developed a new, sensitive camera for the television company RCA. This was called the iconoscope, and it became widely used.

Setbacks

In 1935 Farnsworth won a court case against RCA that proved Zworykin had used his electronic television idea. RCA was ordered to pay Farnsworth money for his invention. However, as a well-established business, RCA delayed payments and was then able to make money from their electronic TVs once Farnsworth's **patent** ran out in 1947.

1928—Baird's mechanical TV sends moving images by **radio waves** across the Atlantic Ocean (see page 12). Baird demonstrates mechanical **3D** TV (see page 26). The first U.S. TV station is started by Charles Jenkins.

1930   1935

Popular machine

During World War II (1939–45), many electronics factories were busy making things for the war, not televisions. However, by the 1950s factories were producing the receivers people wanted to buy, as a wider range of programs were **broadcast**. This included soap operas, such as *Guiding Light*, which ran from 1952 to 2009. Soap operas got their name because they were first sponsored on radio by soap companies!

Watching television became very popular. For example, in 1953 over 44 million Americans watched an episode of the comedy series *I Love Lucy* featuring the birth of Lucy's son. This was over 75 percent of all people with televisions. More people watched this show than watched the swearing in of Dwight Eisenhower as U.S. president the next day.

I Love Lucy was the most popular U.S. TV series of the early 1950s. In this episode, the characters argued about breaking their TV receiver!

1936—Electronic TV broadcasts begin in the United States

1938—RCA makes the first U.S. television sets

1939—Peter Goldmark invents a color TV that uses spinning discs

1935

1940

Color television

Color televisions were first invented in the late 1930s by Peter Goldmark, but most people still watched black-and-white TVs during the 1940s and 1950s. This was because color TVs were very expensive, showed unrealistic colors, and did not work well. By the 1960s, more people were buying improved color TVs. Color **cathode ray tubes** fired three separate **electron** beams through a thin metal grid with thousands of tiny holes, called a shadow mask. The mask directed the electrons against three sorts of dots on the screen that glowed red, blue, or green. The combination of these colored dots, or **pixels**, formed images.

Setbacks

Parts in some early color receivers got very hot. Viewers were told to stay near their TV for an hour after they switched it off, in case their homes caught fire!

This diagram shows how cathode-ray color televisions work.

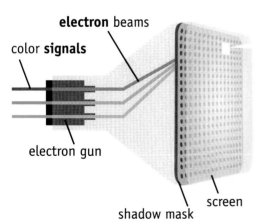

electron beams

shadow mask

screen

phosphor dots

electron beams

color **signals**

electron gun

shadow mask

screen

1944—John Logie Baird invents a completely electronic color TV

1947—Alfred Schroeder invents the shadow mask for color TV

1948—Margaret and John Walson create the first **cable TV** network (see page 20)

Better reception

John and Margaret Walson owned a TV store in Mahanoy City, Pennsylvania, but they sold few receivers because the picture was fuzzy. The hills nearby blocked radio **signals** from reaching their receivers. In 1948 the Walsons fixed an antenna on the top of a nearby mountain, where there was clear TV reception, and laid a cable from this to their store. Locals paid for the Walsons to link their homes to the cable to get a clear picture. This was the first **cable TV**. Today's cable TV companies offer hundreds of channels for customers.

Setbacks

The first TV controls were wired to the television. Later, remote (wireless) controls operated the TV using a flash of light. But other household lights and bright sunlight could accidentally change channels!

This large remote control was used in the 1950s.

Using satellites

There is a limit to how far TV programs can be broadcast by **radio waves**. Radio waves travel in straight lines. They cannot travel around Earth, because it has a curved shape. To send programs worldwide, TV companies beam their programs straight up to TV **satellites**. The satellites then bounce radio signals back to Earth. People with satellite dishes can receive the signals. The first TV satellite, the *Telstar*, was carried to space on a rocket in 1962, but today there are hundreds of them.

Satellite TV made it possible for people to watch live images from the surface of the Moon in 1969.

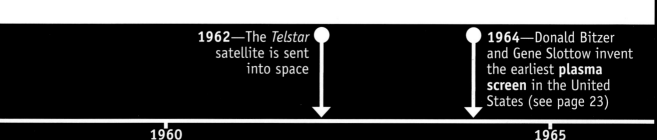

1962—The *Telstar* satellite is sent into space

1964—Donald Bitzer and Gene Slottow invent the earliest **plasma screen** in the United States (see page 23)

1960

1965

Baird's first TV showed images 6 centimeters (2.5 inches) high. Ever since then, **receivers** have generally been getting bigger to show bigger images. Big **cathode ray tube** receivers are bulky, heavy, and use up a lot of **electricity**. Today, all new TV receivers have flat screens. They are light, thin, and energy efficient for their size. Look closely at the surface of a flat screen TV, and you can see it is divided up into millions of **pixels**. Each pixel is made of red, blue, and green **subpixels**. Images are made onscreen when the subpixels flick on or off.

Flat screen TVs can be made much bigger than older cathode-ray tube televisions because they do not need heavy, fragile glass tubes inside.

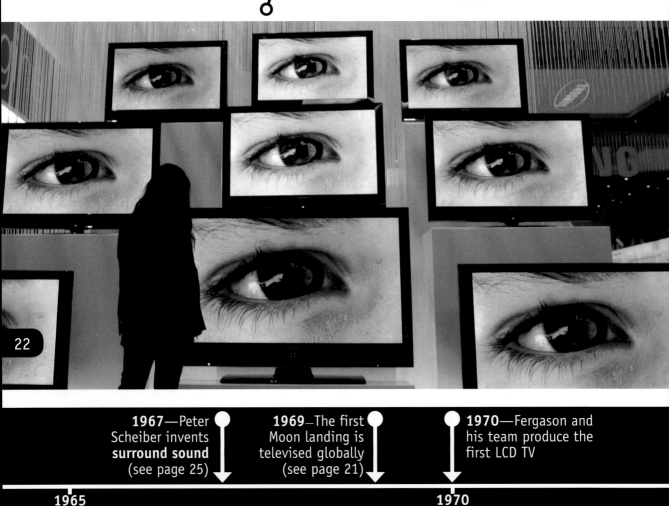

22

1967—Peter Scheiber invents **surround sound** (see page 25)

1969—The first Moon landing is televised globally (see page 21)

1970—Fergason and his team produce the first LCD TV

1965   1970

Two types

There are two main types of flat screens. **Plasma screens** were invented in 1964 by Donald Bitzer and Gene Slottow. The screens use tiny bulbs filled with very hot, glowing gas to light up subpixels. **LCD screens**, which were invented in 1967 by James Fergason, work differently. In LCD screens, the subpixels are like tiny, colored sunglasses in front of a lit-up screen. The amount of light they let through to form an image onscreen depends on a special liquid. This can become more or less **transparent** depending on the size of the **electronic signal**.

subpixels make up image on screen

colored filters

liquid lets through different amounts of light

light source

These are the four main layers of an LCD screen. Electronic signals control how much light is let through the liquid layer.

Setbacks

In early plasma screens, subpixels sometimes stayed permanently black, usually in the shape of a word or other shape that had remained on screen for a long time!

Carrying more information

There are many sizes of **radio waves**, and only some are used to carry television signals. Others are reserved for other purposes, such as for airline pilots to communicate. In the 1990s, countries worldwide realized there would soon be too many channels to fit onto the TV radio waves. They worked together to develop **digital TV**.

With digital TV, programs are converted into computer code that takes up less space than older signals on radio waves. This means the waves can carry more channels. Receivers piece the code back together into programs. In some countries, there are an increasing number of shows in which viewers can also interact with digital TV—for example, by pressing buttons to take part in TV quizzes. By 2010 about 13 countries had switched to **broadcasting** just digital signals.

The Pearl Oriental tower in Shanghai, China, broadcasts digital TV programs.

Home theaters

Watching television today can feel like being in a small movie theater! Many flat screens can display more pixels per square inch to show **high-definition** (HD) images. Some have **surround sound**, invented by Peter Scheiber in 1967. Television signals contain separate image and sound parts. Surround sound is a way to divide up the sound part into different pieces. Each piece makes a separate loudspeaker work. When the loudspeakers are placed around a room, viewers hear the sounds as if they are happening around them.

With better screens, digital signals, and surround sound, people today can enjoy a much richer TV experience than in the past.

Setbacks

Scheiber invited Ray Dolby to his home to show how his surround sound invention worked. Dolby quickly made and marketed something similar. The Dolby company became rich by selling surround sound systems!

INTO THE FUTURE

The newest types of **receivers** on sale are **three-dimensional (3D)** TVs. The first one was introduced in 2010 by Samsung. Programs or movies for 3D TV normally look blurred, because they contain two very slightly different images that almost overlap. If viewers wear special **electronic** glasses, the images overlap into a clear picture. Some 3D screens have special textured screens sending different images to each eye, so that viewers do not need glasses. Inventors are already working on special TV screens that will project colored light from different angles. This creates moving images that can be viewed from different sides.

In the future, what we see coming out of 3D TV screens might be even more realistic than today.

EUREKA!

In 1928 John Logie Baird demonstrated the first 3D TV. He did this by showing slightly different images alternately for the left eye, then right eye, so fast that the viewer saw a 3D image.

1998—Several countries start the **digital TV** switch over

Will channel hopping look like this in the future?

Internet TV

The invention of television has allowed global audiences to experience entertainment, news, and sights from around the world. There are now around 1.5 billion TV receivers on the planet. That is about one for every four people! Television audiences are growing for live events, such as the Olympics. However, many people are now watching recordings of programs on the Internet using computers and cell phones. Some TV channels have started creating programs just for the Internet. The first Internet TV **broadcasts** were made in the late 1990s. In the future, people will be able to surf through thousands of channels and movies on TV receivers at home.

2006—Luxembourg is the first country to broadcast just digital TV

2009—The United States completes the transition to digital

2010—Samsung produces the first electronic 3D **high-definition** TV

TIMELINE

1834
William George Horner invents the zoetrope

1837
Samuel Morse demonstrates an electric **telegraph**

1873
Willoughby Smith and Joseph May accidentally discover that more **electricity** flows through selenium in light than it does in the dark

1938
RCA makes the first U.S. television sets

1936
Electronic TV **broadcasts** begin in the United States

1928
Baird's **mechanical** television sends moving images by radio waves across the Atlantic Ocean. Baird demonstrates mechanical **3D** TV.
The first U.S. TV station is started by Charles Jenkins.

1939
Peter Goldmark invents a color TV that uses spinning discs

1944
John Logie Baird invents a completely electronic color TV

1947
Alfred Schroeder invents the shadow mask for color TV

2010
Samsung produce the first electronic 3D **high-definition** TV

1998
Several countries start the **digital TV** switch over

1970
Fergason and his team produce the first **LCD** TV

1883
Paul Nipkow invents the **Nipkow disc** to **scan** images

1897
J. J. Thomson discovers **electrons**. Ferdinand Braun invents the **cathode ray tube.**

1920
Charles Jenkins sends still images using **radio waves**

1927
Philo Farnsworth invents the first **electronic** television

1925
John Logie Baird demonstrates the first working television to the public. Jenkins transmits his first Radio-Movies.

1923
Zworykin invents the iconoscope

1948
John and Margaret Walson create the first **cable TV** network

1955
Zenith makes the first remote control

1962
The *Telstar* **satellite** is sent into space

1969
The first space landing is televised globally

1967
Peter Scheiber invents **surround sound**

1964
Donald Bitzer and Gene Slottow invent the earliest **plasma screen** in the United States

GLOSSARY

amplifier device used to increase the strength of a signal

broadcast send out a program that can be viewed on TV receivers

cable TV television system in which signals move through wires, not via radio waves

cathode ray tube device in which images are made when electrons hit a glass screen

digital TV television system in which sound and image signals are sent as computer (digital) code

electricity form of energy from the flow of an electric charge

electron tiny particle with a negative charge usually found in an atom

electronic something that works using the flow of electrons

high-definition television system that shows much more detailed images than normal TV

LCD screen stands for "Liquid Crystal Display." This is a flat electronic display panel that filters light to produce an image.

magnet device or object that attracts some metals, such as iron or steel

mechanical describes a machine that works mainly using moving parts—for example, an engine turns wheels in a car

Nipkow disc disc with holes for converting light and dark patterns into signals, and signals into light patterns

patent official proof that an invention, idea, or process was the idea of a particular person, and protection from it being copied

photocell device creating a signal size depending on the amount of light it is exposed to

pixel smallest point or dot making up an image

plasma screen thin, flat electronic display panel using glowing gas bulbs to produce an image

radio wave type of radiation that moves fast and straight like light

receiver device that receives a signal and converts it into sound and images

resolution measure of the detail with which an image appears on a screen, usually shown in pixels or dots per inch

rotate turn around or spin

satellite object put into space to move around Earth, often to transmit radio and other signals

scan change images into patterns of electricity or signals

signal message, usually sent as sound, light, or a radio wave

subpixel building block of a pixel

surround sound system in movie theaters or for televisions that reproduces sound from loudspeakers all around the audience

telegraph system for sending messages by radio waves or electric wires

three-dimensional (3D) having, or seeming to have, height, width, and depth. Real objects are 3D, but pictures on paper are not.

transmitter device that sends out a signal as a radio wave

transparent see-through

FIND OUT MORE

Books

Krull, Kathleen. *The Boy Who Invented TV: The Story of Philo Farnsworth*. New York: Alfred A. Knopf, 2009.

Richter, Joanne. *Inventing the Television* (*Breakthrough Inventions*). New York: Crabtree, 2006.

Teitelbaum, Michael. *Television* (*21st-Century Skills Innovation Library*). Ann Arbor, Mich.: Cherry Lake, 2009.

Websites

www.fcc.gov/cgb/kidszone/faqs_tv.html
This website of the U.S. Federal Communications Commission answers some common questions about television.

www.museum.tv
Find out more about television through this website of the Museum of Broadcast Communications.

www.mztv.com
Enter this virtual museum to learn more about the history of television.

Places to visit

The Museum of Broadcast Communications
360 N. State Street
Chicago, Illinois 60654
www.museum.tv

The Radio and Television Museum
2608 Mitchellville Road
Bowie, Maryland 20716
www.radiohistory.org

INDEX